Intentional Parenting Journal

This journal belongs to the

Write out your family's mission, vision, ethos, goals, and your goals for the children.

Our Mission

Our Vision

Our Ethos

Our Goals

Our Goals for the Children

Train up a child in the way he should go; even when he is old he will not depart from it.
Proverbs 22:6

Introduction

Are you having hard conversations with your children? Are you teaching them the fundamentals? Are you equipping them with tools to navigate through life? Don't let culture, tradition, or the world dictate who they are and how to live. My sons and I often have conversations about several topics, from gender expectations to taking responsibility, contentment, peer pressure, giving, societal expectations, gender roles, family, violence against women, etc. It is crucial to start having these hard conversations. Start talking now. Please don't wait till they become teenagers.

So this past summer, we started

something in my home that completely changed my life. We became intentional about communicating and connecting with our sons. My husband and I started "Okojie Conversations," we created a list of 100 questions and conversation starters and picked one daily to discuss with the boys. That was the best decision I've made as a parent and my most significant time investment since I birthed them.

    The goal was simple, **"TALK WITHOUT JUDGMENT, COMMUNICATE, AND CONNECT."** We typically spend 30 minutes after bible study discussing; we've talked about puberty, guns, found out their thoughts on dating, money, racism, tribalism, etc. This isn't glossy, hiding from real issues. We talk about these things; we allow them to share their thoughts and provide some input, and that's it. Certain lessons are reiterated if needed, but I realized my sons became more comfortable and open. We can talk about almost anything now. Whereas they were hiding certain knowledge before, they can now express themselves better.

I couldn't be more thankful for the opportunity to do this with them. I'd gifted myself the most incredible joy by starting Okojies conversations. It was all I needed to navigate parenthood easily. The year before was tough.

At the beginning of last school year, I'd gotten a call from my son's middle school principal. He had gotten into a verbal altercation with one of his teammates. We'd dropped him off early that day in school, and my sweet little boy had taunted his basketball teammate about how much of a better player he was than him. He went on to say not so many nice things. Mind you, my son had just started playing basketball two months prior, unlike some of the other kids on the team. Suddenly, he's able to make shots and becomes prideful, and not only that, he decides to pick on the one boy he felt he was better than. He hadn't learned how to use his words with grace and not to be puffed up.

I was disappointed and angry. Having to

explain to the principal that we raised him to be kind was something I hated doing. I made that situation about me; I yelled at him and took away his privileges. I never taught him the lessons I'd the opportunity to teach. After that first call, we had a few more calls from school. I soon realized that he constantly tried to prove something and speak his mind. Unfortunately, that got him lots of trouble.

    Confidence is excellent, and delusional confidence can transform your life because it births a high sense of self that others can't easily break. However, as a Christian, I also understand that Everything I am and will be and all I have is given to me by God. Understanding how to use my words with grace and having self-confidence without taunting others or bringing them down was a lesson I had to teach him. This book discusses how my son's behavior made me feel. I was angry at myself and very disappointed with him. I was inspired to write this book because of my experience and navigating the waters of parenting. Everything changed after we became intentional and the calls from school stopped. When raising children, you've got to understand that every child is different, so how you teach and lead them must also be different. This is not about you; it's bigger than you. It requires grace and being intentional.

Besides communicating with our boys, we intentionally connect with them and allow them to explore their gifts and talents. Our intentionality encourages them to transmute their energies into passions that lift their spirits and improve them.

One thing that helped me was I had parents who allowed me to explore. I wasn't into sports, although I ran track in secondary school. I was surrounded by adults who allowed me to expand my mind and explore. My principal in secondary school was one of them, and several teachers along the way. Who pushed me and would speak words into my life that I see manifest.

I am intentional in helping my sons explore

every passion. My first son loves basketball; he spent the entire summer practicing and honing his skills. We enrolled him in two basketball camps this summer and just found a personal coach. Having a child in sports is a lot of work and dedication. He also just signed up for Cross Country. My other son loves Beyblades and sometimes competes in tournaments across the state line.

When it comes to your children, be intentional, laser-focused, and tenaciously help them pursue their dreams and explore. Allow your children to explore! Don't cage their talents or discourage them. I'm my kids' biggest hype man, supporting every dream or passion they have. I invest my time and energy into it and put all I've got into ensuring they succeed in whatever they do. As I constantly encourage them to be the best in everything, I also give them room to change, grow, and fail.

I teach my sons to be vulnerable and share their emotions. We have to allow men to show all their feelings. They are trained not to be angry, cry, show weakness, and be a hard guy all the time. This is unrealistic and sad. The fact a man can't share their pain without being laughed at or judged and called a sissy is sad. I allow my sons to be vulnerable with their emotions. I'm raising my sons to show me how they feel and express their feelings.

Stop saying boys don't cry. They should, and that's okay. Give them the space to express their feelings, ask them questions about how they feel, and allow them to vent and not bottle things up. Stop imposing on them burdens you can't carry. As a parent, focus on communicating, connecting, and allowing them to explore their talents and be in tune with their emotions. Having well-rounded kids is essential and must be a priority.

This journal and the book teach parents about communicating, connecting, and exploring their children's interests. I hope this journal helps as you journey through parenthood.

Note

Use this journal daily as you discuss topics; you can add questions not listed in this journal or make up your own. Keep in mind that these are just samples. You can remove or skip questions you are uncomfortable with or that aren't age-appropriate.

I also included bonus pages to help you record your progress as you communicate, connect, and instruct your child(ren). You can use those weekly, monthly, or as needed.

100 Conversation Starters and

Questions

1. Let's talk about puberty.
2. What are your thoughts on bullying?
3. Let's talk about body image. Does it matter how big or little you are?
4. Do you think smoking is okay?
5. What are your thoughts on drugs?
6. What are your thoughts on guns and shooting in school?
7. What are your thoughts on education and its importance?
8. What are your thoughts on slavery, sexism, tribalism, colorism, and racism?
9. Does skin color matter?
10. What are your thoughts on obeying the

law, authority, police brutality, etc.?
11. What are your thoughts on respect for women? Respect for Men?
12. What are your thoughts on emotional intelligence and how we treat others and handle situations?
13. Is it okay to be delusional about your abilities or have a high sense of self?
14. How we see ourselves matters; what do you think of yourself?
15. Are friendships and relationships important? Should they define our lives?
16. Is success essential, and is it the same as wealth?
17. What are your thoughts on nepotism?
18. Do you ever feel unloved or unheard? When or how?
19. Is physical fitness and activities important?
20. What are your thoughts on taking care of yourself?
21. How important is nutrition to you and

eating?
22. How do you feel when you know someone likes you? Or don't like you?
23. How do you feel when you know you are being heard?
24. How do you feel when you are recognized for something good?
25. What do you want to be when you grow up?
26. What would you love to do with your children when you become a dad or mom?
27. Would you want to get married? Why or why not?
28. Would you want to have children? Why or why not?
29. What is a good age to start dating?
30. What do you know about sex? What is a good age to start having sex?
31. What are your thoughts on people influencing your choices negatively?
32. What is self-esteem?
33. How do you show respect to yourself,

others, and authority?
34. How do you set boundaries?
35. What does cleanliness mean and care for our world and environment?
36. What do you think the role of a mom or wife is?
37. What do you think the role of a dad or husband is?
38. What do you think the role of man and woman is?
39. What are your thoughts on peer pressure?
40. What do you enjoy doing the most?
41. What do you always want to do?
42. If you can be anything, what would you want to be?
43. What are your thoughts on asking for help?
44. What are your thoughts on sharing your time, money, and resources?
45. What are your thoughts on depending on others?
46. What do you think love is?

47. What are your thoughts on violence and gangs, and cliques?
48. What are your thoughts on abortion?
49. What are your thoughts on lying and honesty? What are your thoughts on lying to get out of trouble or to get ahead?
50. What are your thoughts on honest living and doing what you can to be comfortable?
51. What are your thoughts on mental health and its importance?
52. What are your thoughts on depression?
53. What are your thoughts on suicide?
54. What are your thoughts on drinking alcohol, smoking, or vaping?
55. Is beating or hitting a (wo)man okay?
56. What are your thoughts on helping a spouse around the house?
57. What are your thoughts on abstinence?
58. When you notice injustice, what do you do?
59. When dating, is it your responsibility to

take care of the girl/boy?
60. When dating, is it a man's responsibility to take care of you?
61. Is it okay for men to cry?
62. What are your thoughts on homosexuality and LGBTQ?
63. Do you believe God is real? Heaven? Hell?
64. Do you believe we all serve the same God?
65. Is it okay to be friends with people who don't have the same faith as yours?
66. Is it okay to be silent when you see people doing something wrong?
67. No means no! What does that mean? When a girl says no, it means no. Explain what rape is.
68. Talk about wrong and right touches.
69. What are your thoughts on guarding your heart?
70. What are your thoughts on setting priorities?
71. What are your thoughts on setting

goals?
72. What would you do if someone told you to do something terrible?
73. What would you do if someone online asked for your home address or pictures?
74. What should you do if you are online and someone asks for your naked pictures or shares weird images with you?
75. What should you do if someone tells you to sneak out of the house without your parent's approval?
76. What are your thoughts on giving?
77. What are your thoughts on working?
78. What are your thoughts on financial responsibility? Debt, credit, investing, saving, liability, credit scores?
79. What are your thoughts on death and dying?
80. What are your thoughts on material possession and simple or extravagant living?

81. What makes you sad? What should you do when someone is unhappy?
82. What makes you happy? Are you happy?
83. What makes you angry? What can I do as a parent when you are angry?
84. What makes you sad?
85. What irritates you?
86. What activities overwhelm you and make you unhappy?
87. How are you a good citizen of the earth?
88. What new things do you think will make you happy?
89. What would you like to learn?
90. On a scale of 1-10, how am I doing as a parent?
91. What can I do to be a better parent?
92. What can you do to be a better child?
93. On a scale of 1-10, how do you think you are doing as a child?
94. What are your thoughts on entitlement? Does anyone owe

you anything? Do you owe anyone anything?
95. Who contributes to your happiness or unhappiness? Does your family, sibling, friends, teachers, and trainers make you happy or sad?
96. What contributes to your happiness or unhappiness? Does your school, afterschool programs, camp, hobby, sports, and church, make you happy or sad?
97. If you can learn anything, what would it be?
98. Is it okay to tell people everything about you?
99. What do you need beyond the basics that we provide?
100. Do you think the discipline and consequences in our family are fair? Would you change anything? Why?

Conversation Starter Journal

| The topic we discussed: | | Date |

Record your child(ren) response: Share your thoughts

What went well?   What didn't go well

What do you think God is saying about this topic?

_____
_____
_____
_____
_____
_____
_____
_____
_____
_____
_____
_____
_____

What have I learned about my child(ren)?

_____
_____
_____
_____
_____
_____
_____
_____
_____
_____
_____
_____
_____

What have I learned as a parent?

_____
_____
_____
_____
_____
_____
_____
_____
_____
_____
_____
_____
_____

What would I do better next time?

_____
_____
_____
_____
_____
_____
_____
_____
_____
_____
_____
_____
_____

The topic we discussed:		Date

Record your child(ren) response: Share your thoughts

_____   _____
_____   _____
_____   _____
_____   _____
_____   _____
_____   _____
_____   _____
_____   _____
_____   _____
_____   _____

What went well?   What didn't go well

_____   _____
_____   _____
_____   _____
_____   _____
_____   _____
_____   _____
_____   _____
_____   _____
_____   _____
_____   _____

What do you think God is saying about this topic?

_____
_____
_____
_____
_____
_____
_____
_____
_____
_____
_____
_____
_____

What have I learned about my child(ren)?

_____
_____
_____
_____
_____
_____
_____
_____
_____
_____
_____
_____
_____

What have I learned as a parent?

_____
_____
_____
_____
_____
_____
_____
_____
_____
_____
_____
_____
_____

What would I do better next time?

_____
_____
_____
_____
_____
_____
_____
_____
_____
_____
_____
_____
_____

The topic we discussed: | Date

Record your child(ren) response: | Share your thoughts

What went well? | What didn't go well

What do you think God is saying about this topic?	What have I learned about my child(ren)?

What have I learned as a parent?	What would I do better next time?

┌─ The topic we discussed: ──────────┐   ┌─ Date ─┐
│   │   │   │
└────────────────────────────────────┘   └────────┘

Record your child(ren) response: Share your thoughts

_____   _____
_____   _____
_____   _____
_____   _____
_____   _____
_____   _____
_____   _____
_____   _____
_____   _____
_____   _____
_____   _____
_____   _____

What went well?   What didn't go well

_____   _____
_____   _____
_____   _____
_____   _____
_____   _____
_____   _____
_____   _____
_____   _____
_____   _____
_____   _____
_____   _____
_____   _____

What do you think God is saying about this topic?	What have I learned about my child(ren)?

What have I learned as a parent?	What would I do better next time?

┌─ The topic we discussed: ─────────┐   ┌─ Date ─┐
│   │   │   │
└────────────────────────────────────┘   └────────┘

Record your child(ren) response: Share your thoughts

_____   _____
_____   _____
_____   _____
_____   _____
_____   _____
_____   _____
_____   _____
_____   _____
_____   _____
_____   _____
_____   _____
_____   _____

What went well?   What didn't go well

_____   _____
_____   _____
_____   _____
_____   _____
_____   _____
_____   _____
_____   _____
_____   _____
_____   _____
_____   _____
_____   _____
_____   _____

What do you think God is saying about this topic?

_____
_____
_____
_____
_____
_____
_____
_____
_____
_____
_____
_____

What have I learned about my child(ren)?

_____
_____
_____
_____
_____
_____
_____
_____
_____
_____
_____
_____

What have I learned as a parent?

_____
_____
_____
_____
_____
_____
_____
_____
_____
_____
_____
_____

What would I do better next time?

_____
_____
_____
_____
_____
_____
_____
_____
_____
_____
_____
_____

The topic we discussed:

Date

Record your child(ren) response:

Share your thoughts

What went well?

What didn't go well

What do you think God is saying about this topic?

_____
_____
_____
_____
_____
_____
_____
_____
_____
_____
_____
_____
_____

What have I learned about my child(ren)?

_____
_____
_____
_____
_____
_____
_____
_____
_____
_____
_____
_____
_____

What have I learned as a parent?

_____
_____
_____
_____
_____
_____
_____
_____
_____
_____
_____
_____
_____

What would I do better next time?

_____
_____
_____
_____
_____
_____
_____
_____
_____
_____
_____
_____
_____

The topic we discussed: | Date

Record your child(ren) response: | Share your thoughts

What went well? | What didn't go well

What do you think God is saying about this topic?

_____
_____
_____
_____
_____
_____
_____
_____
_____
_____
_____
_____

What have I learned about my child(ren)?

_____
_____
_____
_____
_____
_____
_____
_____
_____
_____
_____
_____

What have I learned as a parent?

_____
_____
_____
_____
_____
_____
_____
_____
_____
_____
_____
_____

What would I do better next time?

_____
_____
_____
_____
_____
_____
_____
_____
_____
_____
_____
_____

The topic we discussed:	Date

Record your child(ren) response:

_____
_____
_____
_____
_____
_____
_____
_____
_____
_____
_____
_____

Share your thoughts

_____
_____
_____
_____
_____
_____
_____
_____
_____
_____
_____
_____

What went well?

_____
_____
_____
_____
_____
_____
_____
_____
_____
_____
_____
_____

What didn't go well

_____
_____
_____
_____
_____
_____
_____
_____
_____
_____
_____
_____

What do you think God is saying about this topic?

_____
_____
_____
_____
_____
_____
_____
_____
_____
_____
_____
_____
_____
_____

What have I learned about my child(ren)?

_____
_____
_____
_____
_____
_____
_____
_____
_____
_____
_____
_____
_____
_____

What have I learned as a parent?

_____
_____
_____
_____
_____
_____
_____
_____
_____
_____
_____
_____
_____
_____

What would I do better next time?

_____
_____
_____
_____
_____
_____
_____
_____
_____
_____
_____
_____
_____
_____

The topic we discussed:	Date

Record your child(ren) response:

Share your thoughts

What went well?

What didn't go well

What do you think God is saying about this topic?

_____
_____
_____
_____
_____
_____
_____
_____
_____
_____
_____
_____
_____

What have I learned about my child(ren)?

_____
_____
_____
_____
_____
_____
_____
_____
_____
_____
_____
_____
_____

What have I learned as a parent?

_____
_____
_____
_____
_____
_____
_____
_____
_____
_____
_____
_____
_____

What would I do better next time?

_____
_____
_____
_____
_____
_____
_____
_____
_____
_____
_____
_____
_____

| The topic we discussed: | Date |

Record your child(ren) response:

Share your thoughts

What went well?

What didn't go well

What do you think God is saying about this topic?

___

What have I learned about my child(ren)?

___

What have I learned as a parent?

___

What would I do better next time?

___

The topic we discussed:

Date

Record your child(ren) response:

Share your thoughts

What went well?

What didn't go well

What do you think God is saying about this topic?

_____
_____
_____
_____
_____
_____
_____
_____
_____
_____
_____
_____
_____

What have I learned about my child(ren)?

_____
_____
_____
_____
_____
_____
_____
_____
_____
_____
_____
_____
_____

What have I learned as a parent?

_____
_____
_____
_____
_____
_____
_____
_____
_____
_____
_____
_____
_____

What would I do better next time?

_____
_____
_____
_____
_____
_____
_____
_____
_____
_____
_____
_____
_____

The topic we discussed:	Date

Record your child(ren) response:

_____
_____
_____
_____
_____
_____
_____
_____
_____
_____
_____
_____
_____

Share your thoughts

_____
_____
_____
_____
_____
_____
_____
_____
_____
_____
_____
_____
_____

What went well?

_____
_____
_____
_____
_____
_____
_____
_____
_____
_____
_____
_____

What didn't go well

_____
_____
_____
_____
_____
_____
_____
_____
_____
_____
_____
_____

What do you think God is saying about this topic?

_____
_____
_____
_____
_____
_____
_____
_____
_____
_____
_____
_____
_____

What have I learned about my child(ren)?

_____
_____
_____
_____
_____
_____
_____
_____
_____
_____
_____
_____
_____

What have I learned as a parent?

_____
_____
_____
_____
_____
_____
_____
_____
_____
_____
_____
_____
_____

What would I do better next time?

_____
_____
_____
_____
_____
_____
_____
_____
_____
_____
_____
_____
_____

The topic we discussed:

Date

Record your child(ren) response:

Share your thoughts

What went well?

What didn't go well

What do you think God is saying about this topic?

_____
_____
_____
_____
_____
_____
_____
_____
_____
_____
_____
_____

What have I learned about my child(ren)?

_____
_____
_____
_____
_____
_____
_____
_____
_____
_____
_____
_____

What have I learned as a parent?

_____
_____
_____
_____
_____
_____
_____
_____
_____
_____
_____
_____

What would I do better next time?

_____
_____
_____
_____
_____
_____
_____
_____
_____
_____
_____
_____

The topic we discussed: **Date**

Record your child(ren) response: Share your thoughts

What went well?   What didn't go well

What do you think God is saying about this topic?

_____
_____
_____
_____
_____
_____
_____
_____
_____
_____
_____
_____

What have I learned about my child(ren)?

_____
_____
_____
_____
_____
_____
_____
_____
_____
_____
_____
_____

What have I learned as a parent?

_____
_____
_____
_____
_____
_____
_____
_____
_____
_____
_____
_____

What would I do better next time?

_____
_____
_____
_____
_____
_____
_____
_____
_____
_____
_____
_____

The topic we discussed: | Date

Record your child(ren) response: | Share your thoughts

What went well? | What didn't go well

What do you think God is saying about this topic?

_____
_____
_____
_____
_____
_____
_____
_____
_____
_____
_____
_____
_____

What have I learned about my child(ren)?

_____
_____
_____
_____
_____
_____
_____
_____
_____
_____
_____
_____
_____

What have I learned as a parent?

_____
_____
_____
_____
_____
_____
_____
_____
_____
_____
_____
_____
_____

What would I do better next time?

_____
_____
_____
_____
_____
_____
_____
_____
_____
_____
_____
_____
_____

The topic we discussed: **Date**

Record your child(ren) response: Share your thoughts

What went well?   What didn't go well

What do you think God is saying about this topic?

_____
_____
_____
_____
_____
_____
_____
_____
_____
_____
_____
_____
_____

What have I learned about my child(ren)?

_____
_____
_____
_____
_____
_____
_____
_____
_____
_____
_____
_____
_____

What have I learned as a parent?

_____
_____
_____
_____
_____
_____
_____
_____
_____
_____
_____
_____
_____

What would I do better next time?

_____
_____
_____
_____
_____
_____
_____
_____
_____
_____
_____
_____
_____

The topic we discussed:

Date

Record your child(ren) response:

Share your thoughts

What went well?

What didn't go well

What do you think God is saying about this topic?

_____
_____
_____
_____
_____
_____
_____
_____
_____
_____
_____
_____
_____
_____

What have I learned about my child(ren)?

_____
_____
_____
_____
_____
_____
_____
_____
_____
_____
_____
_____
_____
_____

What have I learned as a parent?

_____
_____
_____
_____
_____
_____
_____
_____
_____
_____
_____
_____
_____
_____

What would I do better next time?

_____
_____
_____
_____
_____
_____
_____
_____
_____
_____
_____
_____
_____
_____

The topic we discussed:		Date

Record your child(ren) response:

Share your thoughts

What went well?

What didn't go well

What do you think God is saying about this topic?	What have I learned about my child(ren)?

What have I learned as a parent?	What would I do better next time?

The topic we discussed:	Date

Record your child(ren) response:

Share your thoughts

What went well?

What didn't go well

What do you think God is saying about this topic?

_____
_____
_____
_____
_____
_____
_____
_____
_____
_____
_____
_____
_____
_____

What have I learned about my child(ren)?

_____
_____
_____
_____
_____
_____
_____
_____
_____
_____
_____
_____
_____
_____

What have I learned as a parent?

_____
_____
_____
_____
_____
_____
_____
_____
_____
_____
_____
_____
_____
_____

What would I do better next time?

_____
_____
_____
_____
_____
_____
_____
_____
_____
_____
_____
_____
_____
_____

The topic we discussed: Date

Record your child(ren) response: Share your thoughts

What went well?   What didn't go well

What do you think God is saying about this topic?

_____
_____
_____
_____
_____
_____
_____
_____
_____
_____
_____
_____
_____
_____

What have I learned about my child(ren)?

_____
_____
_____
_____
_____
_____
_____
_____
_____
_____
_____
_____
_____
_____

What have I learned as a parent?

_____
_____
_____
_____
_____
_____
_____
_____
_____
_____
_____
_____
_____
_____

What would I do better next time?

_____
_____
_____
_____
_____
_____
_____
_____
_____
_____
_____
_____
_____
_____

The topic we discussed: | Date

Record your child(ren) response: Share your thoughts

What went well?   What didn't go well

What do you think God is saying about this topic?

_____
_____
_____
_____
_____
_____
_____
_____
_____
_____
_____
_____

What have I learned about my child(ren)?

_____
_____
_____
_____
_____
_____
_____
_____
_____
_____
_____
_____

What have I learned as a parent?

_____
_____
_____
_____
_____
_____
_____
_____
_____
_____
_____
_____

What would I do better next time?

_____
_____
_____
_____
_____
_____
_____
_____
_____
_____
_____
_____

The topic we discussed: **Date**

Record your child(ren) response: Share your thoughts

What went well? What didn't go well

What do you think God is saying about this topic?
_____
_____
_____
_____
_____
_____
_____
_____
_____
_____
_____
_____

What have I learned about my child(ren)?
_____
_____
_____
_____
_____
_____
_____
_____
_____
_____
_____
_____

What have I learned as a parent?
_____
_____
_____
_____
_____
_____
_____
_____
_____
_____
_____
_____

What would I do better next time?
_____
_____
_____
_____
_____
_____
_____
_____
_____
_____
_____
_____

The topic we discussed:	Date

Record your child(ren) response:

Share your thoughts

What went well?

What didn't go well

What do you think God is saying about this topic?
_____
_____
_____
_____
_____
_____
_____
_____
_____
_____
_____
_____
_____

What have I learned about my child(ren)?
_____
_____
_____
_____
_____
_____
_____
_____
_____
_____
_____
_____
_____

What have I learned as a parent?
_____
_____
_____
_____
_____
_____
_____
_____
_____
_____
_____
_____
_____

What would I do better next time?
_____
_____
_____
_____
_____
_____
_____
_____
_____
_____
_____
_____
_____

The topic we discussed:		Date

Record your child(ren) response:

Share your thoughts

What went well?

What didn't go well

What do you think God is saying about this topic?

_____
_____
_____
_____
_____
_____
_____
_____
_____
_____
_____
_____
_____

What have I learned about my child(ren)?

_____
_____
_____
_____
_____
_____
_____
_____
_____
_____
_____
_____
_____

What have I learned as a parent?

_____
_____
_____
_____
_____
_____
_____
_____
_____
_____
_____
_____
_____

What would I do better next time?

_____
_____
_____
_____
_____
_____
_____
_____
_____
_____
_____
_____
_____

The topic we discussed: | Date

Record your child(ren) response: | Share your thoughts

What went well? | What didn't go well

What do you think God is saying about this topic?

What have I learned about my child(ren)?

What have I learned as a parent?

What would I do better next time?

The topic we discussed: **Date**

Record your child(ren) response: Share your thoughts

What went well?   What didn't go well

What do you think God is saying about this topic?

_____
_____
_____
_____
_____
_____
_____
_____
_____
_____
_____
_____
_____
_____

What have I learned about my child(ren)?

_____
_____
_____
_____
_____
_____
_____
_____
_____
_____
_____
_____
_____
_____

What have I learned as a parent?

_____
_____
_____
_____
_____
_____
_____
_____
_____
_____
_____
_____
_____
_____

What would I do better next time?

_____
_____
_____
_____
_____
_____
_____
_____
_____
_____
_____
_____
_____
_____

The topic we discussed:	Date

Record your child(ren) response:

Share your thoughts

What went well?

What didn't go well

What do you think God is saying about this topic?	What have I learned about my child(ren)?

What have I learned as a parent?	What would I do better next time?

The topic we discussed:	Date

Record your child(ren) response:

Share your thoughts

What went well?

What didn't go well

What do you think God is saying about this topic?	What have I learned about my child(ren)?

What have I learned as a parent?	What would I do better next time?

The topic we discussed:	Date

Record your child(ren) response: Share your thoughts

What went well?   What didn't go well

What do you think God is saying about this topic?

_____
_____
_____
_____
_____
_____
_____
_____
_____
_____
_____
_____
_____

What have I learned about my child(ren)?

_____
_____
_____
_____
_____
_____
_____
_____
_____
_____
_____
_____
_____

What have I learned as a parent?

_____
_____
_____
_____
_____
_____
_____
_____
_____
_____
_____
_____
_____

What would I do better next time?

_____
_____
_____
_____
_____
_____
_____
_____
_____
_____
_____
_____
_____

The topic we discussed:	Date

Record your child(ren) response:

Share your thoughts

What went well?

What didn't go well

What do you think God is saying about this topic?	What have I learned about my child(ren)?
_____	_____
_____	_____
_____	_____
_____	_____
_____	_____
_____	_____
_____	_____
_____	_____
_____	_____
_____	_____
_____	_____
_____	_____

What have I learned as a parent?	What would I do better next time?
_____	_____
_____	_____
_____	_____
_____	_____
_____	_____
_____	_____
_____	_____
_____	_____
_____	_____
_____	_____
_____	_____
_____	_____

The topic we discussed: | **Date**

Record your child(ren) response:

Share your thoughts

What went well?

What didn't go well

What do you think God is saying about this topic?

_____
_____
_____
_____
_____
_____
_____
_____
_____
_____
_____
_____
_____

What have I learned about my child(ren)?

_____
_____
_____
_____
_____
_____
_____
_____
_____
_____
_____
_____
_____

What have I learned as a parent?

_____
_____
_____
_____
_____
_____
_____
_____
_____
_____
_____
_____
_____

What would I do better next time?

_____
_____
_____
_____
_____
_____
_____
_____
_____
_____
_____
_____
_____

The topic we discussed:	Date

Record your child(ren) response:

Share your thoughts

What went well?

What didn't go well

What do you think God is saying about this topic?	What have I learned about my child(ren)?

What have I learned as a parent?	What would I do better next time?

The topic we discussed: **Date**

Record your child(ren) response: Share your thoughts

_____   _____
_____   _____
_____   _____
_____   _____
_____   _____
_____   _____
_____   _____
_____   _____
_____   _____
_____   _____

What went well?   What didn't go well

_____   _____
_____   _____
_____   _____
_____   _____
_____   _____
_____   _____
_____   _____
_____   _____
_____   _____
_____   _____

What do you think God is saying about this topic?

What have I learned about my child(ren)?

What have I learned as a parent?

What would I do better next time?

The topic we discussed: | **Date**

Record your child(ren) response:

Share your thoughts

What went well?

What didn't go well

What do you think God is saying about this topic?

_____
_____
_____
_____
_____
_____
_____
_____
_____
_____
_____
_____

What have I learned about my child(ren)?

_____
_____
_____
_____
_____
_____
_____
_____
_____
_____
_____
_____

What have I learned as a parent?

_____
_____
_____
_____
_____
_____
_____
_____
_____
_____
_____
_____

What would I do better next time?

_____
_____
_____
_____
_____
_____
_____
_____
_____
_____
_____
_____

The topic we discussed: | Date

Record your child(ren) response: | Share your thoughts

What went well? | What didn't go well

What do you think God is saying about this topic?

_____
_____
_____
_____
_____
_____
_____
_____
_____
_____
_____
_____
_____

What have I learned about my child(ren)?

_____
_____
_____
_____
_____
_____
_____
_____
_____
_____
_____
_____
_____

What have I learned as a parent?

_____
_____
_____
_____
_____
_____
_____
_____
_____
_____
_____
_____
_____

What would I do better next time?

_____
_____
_____
_____
_____
_____
_____
_____
_____
_____
_____
_____
_____

The topic we discussed:		Date

Record your child(ren) response:

Share your thoughts

What went well?

What didn't go well

What do you think God is saying about this topic?

_____
_____
_____
_____
_____
_____
_____
_____
_____
_____
_____
_____

What have I learned about my child(ren)?

_____
_____
_____
_____
_____
_____
_____
_____
_____
_____
_____
_____

What have I learned as a parent?

_____
_____
_____
_____
_____
_____
_____
_____
_____
_____
_____
_____

What would I do better next time?

_____
_____
_____
_____
_____
_____
_____
_____
_____
_____
_____
_____

The topic we discussed:	Date

Record your child(ren) response:

_____
_____
_____
_____
_____
_____
_____
_____
_____
_____
_____
_____

Share your thoughts

_____
_____
_____
_____
_____
_____
_____
_____
_____
_____
_____
_____

What went well?

_____
_____
_____
_____
_____
_____
_____
_____
_____
_____
_____
_____

What didn't go well

_____
_____
_____
_____
_____
_____
_____
_____
_____
_____
_____
_____

What do you think God is saying about this topic?

_____
_____
_____
_____
_____
_____
_____
_____
_____
_____
_____
_____
_____
_____

What have I learned about my child(ren)?

_____
_____
_____
_____
_____
_____
_____
_____
_____
_____
_____
_____
_____
_____

What have I learned as a parent?

_____
_____
_____
_____
_____
_____
_____
_____
_____
_____
_____
_____
_____
_____

What would I do better next time?

_____
_____
_____
_____
_____
_____
_____
_____
_____
_____
_____
_____
_____
_____

The topic we discussed: | Date

Record your child(ren) response: | Share your thoughts

What went well? | What didn't go well

What do you think God is saying about this topic?

_____
_____
_____
_____
_____
_____
_____
_____
_____
_____
_____
_____
_____

What have I learned about my child(ren)?

_____
_____
_____
_____
_____
_____
_____
_____
_____
_____
_____
_____
_____

What have I learned as a parent?

_____
_____
_____
_____
_____
_____
_____
_____
_____
_____
_____
_____
_____

What would I do better next time?

_____
_____
_____
_____
_____
_____
_____
_____
_____
_____
_____
_____
_____

The topic we discussed: **Date**

Record your child(ren) response: Share your thoughts

What went well?   What didn't go well

What do you think God is saying about this topic?

_____
_____
_____
_____
_____
_____
_____
_____
_____
_____
_____
_____

What have I learned about my child(ren)?

_____
_____
_____
_____
_____
_____
_____
_____
_____
_____
_____
_____

What have I learned as a parent?

_____
_____
_____
_____
_____
_____
_____
_____
_____
_____
_____
_____

What would I do better next time?

_____
_____
_____
_____
_____
_____
_____
_____
_____
_____
_____
_____

| The topic we discussed: | Date |

Record your child(ren) response:

_____
_____
_____
_____
_____
_____
_____
_____
_____
_____
_____
_____
_____

Share your thoughts

_____
_____
_____
_____
_____
_____
_____
_____
_____
_____
_____
_____
_____

What went well?

_____
_____
_____
_____
_____
_____
_____
_____
_____
_____
_____
_____
_____

What didn't go well

_____
_____
_____
_____
_____
_____
_____
_____
_____
_____
_____
_____
_____

What do you think God is saying about this topic?

_____
_____
_____
_____
_____
_____
_____
_____
_____
_____
_____
_____

What have I learned about my child(ren)?

_____
_____
_____
_____
_____
_____
_____
_____
_____
_____
_____
_____

What have I learned as a parent?

_____
_____
_____
_____
_____
_____
_____
_____
_____
_____
_____
_____

What would I do better next time?

_____
_____
_____
_____
_____
_____
_____
_____
_____
_____
_____
_____

| The topic we discussed: | | Date |

Record your child(ren) response: Share your thoughts

What went well?   What didn't go well

What do you think God is saying about this topic?

_____
_____
_____
_____
_____
_____
_____
_____
_____
_____
_____
_____

What have I learned about my child(ren)?

_____
_____
_____
_____
_____
_____
_____
_____
_____
_____
_____
_____

What have I learned as a parent?

_____
_____
_____
_____
_____
_____
_____
_____
_____
_____
_____
_____

What would I do better next time?

_____
_____
_____
_____
_____
_____
_____
_____
_____
_____
_____
_____

The topic we discussed: | Date

Record your child(ren) response: | Share your thoughts

What went well? | What didn't go well

What do you think God is saying about this topic?

_____
_____
_____
_____
_____
_____
_____
_____
_____
_____
_____
_____

What have I learned about my child(ren)?

_____
_____
_____
_____
_____
_____
_____
_____
_____
_____
_____
_____

What have I learned as a parent?

_____
_____
_____
_____
_____
_____
_____
_____
_____
_____
_____
_____
_____

What would I do better next time?

_____
_____
_____
_____
_____
_____
_____
_____
_____
_____
_____
_____
_____

The topic we discussed:

Date

Record your child(ren) response:

Share your thoughts

What went well?

What didn't go well

What do you think God is saying about this topic?

_____
_____
_____
_____
_____
_____
_____
_____
_____
_____
_____
_____
_____

What have I learned about my child(ren)?

_____
_____
_____
_____
_____
_____
_____
_____
_____
_____
_____
_____
_____

What have I learned as a parent?

_____
_____
_____
_____
_____
_____
_____
_____
_____
_____
_____
_____
_____

What would I do better next time?

_____
_____
_____
_____
_____
_____
_____
_____
_____
_____
_____
_____
_____

┌─ The topic we discussed: ─────────┐　　　　┌─ Date ─┐
│   │　　　　│   │
└───────────────────────────────────┘　　　　└────────┘

Record your child(ren) response: Share your thoughts

_____   _____
_____   _____
_____   _____
_____   _____
_____   _____
_____   _____
_____   _____
_____   _____
_____   _____
_____   _____
_____   _____
_____   _____

What went well?   What didn't go well

_____   _____
_____   _____
_____   _____
_____   _____
_____   _____
_____   _____
_____   _____
_____   _____
_____   _____
_____   _____
_____   _____
_____   _____

What do you think God is saying about this topic?

_____
_____
_____
_____
_____
_____
_____
_____
_____
_____
_____
_____
_____

What have I learned about my child(ren)?

_____
_____
_____
_____
_____
_____
_____
_____
_____
_____
_____
_____
_____

What have I learned as a parent?

_____
_____
_____
_____
_____
_____
_____
_____
_____
_____
_____
_____
_____

What would I do better next time?

_____
_____
_____
_____
_____
_____
_____
_____
_____
_____
_____
_____
_____

The topic we discussed: | **Date**

Record your child(ren) response:

Share your thoughts

What went well?

What didn't go well

What do you think God is saying about this topic?

_____
_____
_____
_____
_____
_____
_____
_____
_____
_____
_____
_____

What have I learned about my child(ren)?

_____
_____
_____
_____
_____
_____
_____
_____
_____
_____
_____
_____

What have I learned as a parent?

_____
_____
_____
_____
_____
_____
_____
_____
_____
_____
_____
_____

What would I do better next time?

_____
_____
_____
_____
_____
_____
_____
_____
_____
_____
_____
_____

| The topic we discussed: | Date |

Record your child(ren) response:

Share your thoughts

What went well?

What didn't go well

What do you think God is saying about this topic?

_____
_____
_____
_____
_____
_____
_____
_____
_____
_____
_____
_____

What have I learned about my child(ren)?

_____
_____
_____
_____
_____
_____
_____
_____
_____
_____
_____
_____

What have I learned as a parent?

_____
_____
_____
_____
_____
_____
_____
_____
_____
_____
_____
_____

What would I do better next time?

_____
_____
_____
_____
_____
_____
_____
_____
_____
_____
_____
_____

The topic we discussed: | **Date**

Record your child(ren) response: | Share your thoughts

What went well? | What didn't go well

What do you think God is saying about this topic?	What have I learned about my child(ren)?

What have I learned as a parent?	What would I do better next time?

The topic we discussed: **Date**

Record your child(ren) response: Share your thoughts

What went well?   What didn't go well

What do you think God is saying about this topic?

_____
_____
_____
_____
_____
_____
_____
_____
_____
_____
_____
_____
_____

What have I learned about my child(ren)?

_____
_____
_____
_____
_____
_____
_____
_____
_____
_____
_____
_____
_____

What have I learned as a parent?

_____
_____
_____
_____
_____
_____
_____
_____
_____
_____
_____
_____
_____

What would I do better next time?

_____
_____
_____
_____
_____
_____
_____
_____
_____
_____
_____
_____
_____

| The topic we discussed: | Date |

Record your child(ren) response:

Share your thoughts

_____
_____
_____
_____
_____
_____
_____
_____
_____
_____
_____
_____
_____

What went well?

What didn't go well

_____
_____
_____
_____
_____
_____
_____
_____
_____
_____
_____
_____

What do you think God is saying about this topic?

_____
_____
_____
_____
_____
_____
_____
_____
_____
_____
_____
_____

What have I learned about my child(ren)?

_____
_____
_____
_____
_____
_____
_____
_____
_____
_____
_____
_____

What have I learned as a parent?

_____
_____
_____
_____
_____
_____
_____
_____
_____
_____
_____
_____

What would I do better next time?

_____
_____
_____
_____
_____
_____
_____
_____
_____
_____
_____
_____

The topic we discussed:

Date

Record your child(ren) response:

Share your thoughts

What went well?

What didn't go well

What do you think God is saying about this topic?

_____
_____
_____
_____
_____
_____
_____
_____
_____
_____
_____
_____

What have I learned about my child(ren)?

_____
_____
_____
_____
_____
_____
_____
_____
_____
_____
_____
_____

What have I learned as a parent?

_____
_____
_____
_____
_____
_____
_____
_____
_____
_____
_____
_____

What would I do better next time?

_____
_____
_____
_____
_____
_____
_____
_____
_____
_____
_____
_____

The topic we discussed:	Date

Record your child(ren) response:

Share your thoughts

What went well?

What didn't go well

What do you think God is saying about this topic?

_____
_____
_____
_____
_____
_____
_____
_____
_____
_____
_____
_____

What have I learned about my child(ren)?

_____
_____
_____
_____
_____
_____
_____
_____
_____
_____
_____
_____

What have I learned as a parent?

_____
_____
_____
_____
_____
_____
_____
_____
_____
_____
_____
_____

What would I do better next time?

_____
_____
_____
_____
_____
_____
_____
_____
_____
_____
_____
_____

| The topic we discussed: | Date |

Record your child(ren) response:

Share your thoughts

What went well?

What didn't go well

What do you think God is saying about this topic?

_____
_____
_____
_____
_____
_____
_____
_____
_____
_____
_____
_____

What have I learned about my child(ren)?

_____
_____
_____
_____
_____
_____
_____
_____
_____
_____
_____
_____

What have I learned as a parent?

_____
_____
_____
_____
_____
_____
_____
_____
_____
_____
_____
_____

What would I do better next time?

_____
_____
_____
_____
_____
_____
_____
_____
_____
_____
_____
_____

The topic we discussed:	Date

Record your child(ren) response:

Share your thoughts

What went well?

What didn't go well

What do you think God is saying about this topic?

_____
_____
_____
_____
_____
_____
_____
_____
_____
_____
_____
_____
_____

What have I learned about my child(ren)?

_____
_____
_____
_____
_____
_____
_____
_____
_____
_____
_____
_____
_____

What have I learned as a parent?

_____
_____
_____
_____
_____
_____
_____
_____
_____
_____
_____
_____
_____

What would I do better next time?

_____
_____
_____
_____
_____
_____
_____
_____
_____
_____
_____
_____
_____

The topic we discussed:		Date

Record your child(ren) response:

Share your thoughts

What went well?

What didn't go well

What do you think God is saying about this topic?

What have I learned about my child(ren)?

What have I learned as a parent?

What would I do better next time?

The topic we discussed:	Date

Record your child(ren) response: Share your thoughts

What went well?   What didn't go well

What do you think God is saying about this topic?

_____
_____
_____
_____
_____
_____
_____
_____
_____
_____
_____
_____

What have I learned about my child(ren)?

_____
_____
_____
_____
_____
_____
_____
_____
_____
_____
_____
_____

What have I learned as a parent?

_____
_____
_____
_____
_____
_____
_____
_____
_____
_____
_____
_____

What would I do better next time?

_____
_____
_____
_____
_____
_____
_____
_____
_____
_____
_____
_____

The topic we discussed: **Date**

Record your child(ren) response:　　　Share your thoughts

What went well?　　　What didn't go well

What do you think God is saying about this topic?

_____
_____
_____
_____
_____
_____
_____
_____
_____
_____
_____
_____
_____

What have I learned about my child(ren)?

_____
_____
_____
_____
_____
_____
_____
_____
_____
_____
_____
_____
_____

What have I learned as a parent?

_____
_____
_____
_____
_____
_____
_____
_____
_____
_____
_____
_____
_____

What would I do better next time?

_____
_____
_____
_____
_____
_____
_____
_____
_____
_____
_____
_____
_____

The topic we discussed:	Date

Record your child(ren) response: Share your thoughts

_____   _____
_____   _____
_____   _____
_____   _____
_____   _____
_____   _____
_____   _____
_____   _____
_____   _____
_____   _____
_____   _____

What went well? What didn't go well

_____   _____
_____   _____
_____   _____
_____   _____
_____   _____
_____   _____
_____   _____
_____   _____
_____   _____
_____   _____
_____   _____

What do you think God is saying about this topic?

_____
_____
_____
_____
_____
_____
_____
_____
_____
_____
_____
_____

What have I learned about my child(ren)?

_____
_____
_____
_____
_____
_____
_____
_____
_____
_____
_____
_____

What have I learned as a parent?

_____
_____
_____
_____
_____
_____
_____
_____
_____
_____
_____
_____

What would I do better next time?

_____
_____
_____
_____
_____
_____
_____
_____
_____
_____
_____
_____

The topic we discussed: | **Date**

Record your child(ren) response:

Share your thoughts

What went well?

What didn't go well

What do you think God is saying about this topic?

What have I learned about my child(ren)?

What have I learned as a parent?

What would I do better next time?

The topic we discussed:	Date

Record your child(ren) response: Share your thoughts

What went well?   What didn't go well

What do you think God is saying about this topic?

What have I learned about my child(ren)?

What have I learned as a parent?

What would I do better next time?

The topic we discussed: **Date**

Record your child(ren) response:

Share your thoughts

What went well?

What didn't go well

What do you think God is saying about this topic?

_____
_____
_____
_____
_____
_____
_____
_____
_____
_____
_____
_____

What have I learned about my child(ren)?

_____
_____
_____
_____
_____
_____
_____
_____
_____
_____
_____
_____

What have I learned as a parent?

_____
_____
_____
_____
_____
_____
_____
_____
_____
_____
_____
_____

What would I do better next time?

_____
_____
_____
_____
_____
_____
_____
_____
_____
_____
_____
_____

The topic we discussed:		Date

Record your child(ren) response:

Share your thoughts

What went well?

What didn't go well

What do you think God is saying about this topic?

_____
_____
_____
_____
_____
_____
_____
_____
_____
_____
_____
_____

What have I learned about my child(ren)?

_____
_____
_____
_____
_____
_____
_____
_____
_____
_____
_____
_____

What have I learned as a parent?

_____
_____
_____
_____
_____
_____
_____
_____
_____
_____
_____
_____

What would I do better next time?

_____
_____
_____
_____
_____
_____
_____
_____
_____
_____
_____
_____

The topic we discussed:	Date

Record your child(ren) response:

Share your thoughts

What went well?

What didn't go well

What do you think God is saying about this topic?

_____
_____
_____
_____
_____
_____
_____
_____
_____
_____
_____
_____
_____
_____

What have I learned about my child(ren)?

_____
_____
_____
_____
_____
_____
_____
_____
_____
_____
_____
_____
_____
_____

What have I learned as a parent?

_____
_____
_____
_____
_____
_____
_____
_____
_____
_____
_____
_____
_____
_____

What would I do better next time?

_____
_____
_____
_____
_____
_____
_____
_____
_____
_____
_____
_____
_____
_____

The topic we discussed:	Date

Record your child(ren) response:

Share your thoughts

What went well?

What didn't go well

What do you think God is saying about this topic?	What have I learned about my child(ren)?

What have I learned as a parent?	What would I do better next time?

The topic we discussed: | **Date**

Record your child(ren) response:

Share your thoughts

What went well?

What didn't go well

What do you think God is saying about this topic?	What have I learned about my child(ren)?

What have I learned as a parent?	What would I do better next time?

| The topic we discussed: | Date |

Record your child(ren) response: Share your thoughts

What went well?   What didn't go well

What do you think God is saying about this topic?	What have I learned about my child(ren)?

What have I learned as a parent?	What would I do better next time?

The topic we discussed:

Date

Record your child(ren) response:

Share your thoughts

What went well?

What didn't go well

What do you think God is saying about this topic?

_____
_____
_____
_____
_____
_____
_____
_____
_____
_____
_____
_____

What have I learned about my child(ren)?

_____
_____
_____
_____
_____
_____
_____
_____
_____
_____
_____
_____

What have I learned as a parent?

_____
_____
_____
_____
_____
_____
_____
_____
_____
_____
_____
_____

What would I do better next time?

_____
_____
_____
_____
_____
_____
_____
_____
_____
_____
_____
_____

The topic we discussed: | **Date**

Record your child(ren) response: | Share your thoughts

What went well? | What didn't go well

What do you think God is saying about this topic?

_____
_____
_____
_____
_____
_____
_____
_____
_____
_____
_____
_____
_____

What have I learned about my child(ren)?

_____
_____
_____
_____
_____
_____
_____
_____
_____
_____
_____
_____
_____

What have I learned as a parent?

_____
_____
_____
_____
_____
_____
_____
_____
_____
_____
_____
_____
_____

What would I do better next time?

_____
_____
_____
_____
_____
_____
_____
_____
_____
_____
_____
_____
_____

| The topic we discussed: | Date |

Record your child(ren) response:

Share your thoughts

What went well?

What didn't go well

What do you think God is saying about this topic?

_____
_____
_____
_____
_____
_____
_____
_____
_____
_____
_____
_____
_____

What have I learned about my child(ren)?

_____
_____
_____
_____
_____
_____
_____
_____
_____
_____
_____
_____
_____

What have I learned as a parent?

_____
_____
_____
_____
_____
_____
_____
_____
_____
_____
_____
_____
_____

What would I do better next time?

_____
_____
_____
_____
_____
_____
_____
_____
_____
_____
_____
_____
_____

The topic we discussed: **Date**

Record your child(ren) response:　　　　Share your thoughts

What went well?　　　　　　　　　What didn't go well

What do you think God is saying about this topic?	What have I learned about my child(ren)?

What have I learned as a parent?	What would I do better next time?

The topic we discussed: | Date

Record your child(ren) response: | Share your thoughts

What went well? | What didn't go well

What do you think God is saying about this topic?

_____
_____
_____
_____
_____
_____
_____
_____
_____
_____
_____
_____
_____

What have I learned about my child(ren)?

_____
_____
_____
_____
_____
_____
_____
_____
_____
_____
_____
_____
_____

What have I learned as a parent?

_____
_____
_____
_____
_____
_____
_____
_____
_____
_____
_____
_____
_____

What would I do better next time?

_____
_____
_____
_____
_____
_____
_____
_____
_____
_____
_____
_____
_____

The topic we discussed:	Date

Record your child(ren) response:

Share your thoughts

_____
_____
_____
_____
_____
_____
_____
_____
_____
_____
_____
_____

_____
_____
_____
_____
_____
_____
_____
_____
_____
_____
_____
_____

What went well?

What didn't go well

_____
_____
_____
_____
_____
_____
_____
_____
_____
_____
_____

_____
_____
_____
_____
_____
_____
_____
_____
_____
_____
_____

What do you think God is saying about this topic?

_____
_____
_____
_____
_____
_____
_____
_____
_____
_____
_____
_____
_____

What have I learned about my child(ren)?

_____
_____
_____
_____
_____
_____
_____
_____
_____
_____
_____
_____
_____

What have I learned as a parent?

_____
_____
_____
_____
_____
_____
_____
_____
_____
_____
_____
_____
_____

What would I do better next time?

_____
_____
_____
_____
_____
_____
_____
_____
_____
_____
_____
_____
_____

The topic we discussed:	Date

Record your child(ren) response:

Share your thoughts

_____
_____
_____
_____
_____
_____
_____
_____
_____
_____
_____
_____

_____
_____
_____
_____
_____
_____
_____
_____
_____
_____
_____
_____

What went well?

What didn't go well

_____
_____
_____
_____
_____
_____
_____
_____
_____
_____
_____
_____
_____

_____
_____
_____
_____
_____
_____
_____
_____
_____
_____
_____
_____
_____

What do you think God is saying about this topic?

_____
_____
_____
_____
_____
_____
_____
_____
_____
_____
_____
_____
_____

What have I learned about my child(ren)?

_____
_____
_____
_____
_____
_____
_____
_____
_____
_____
_____
_____
_____

What have I learned as a parent?

_____
_____
_____
_____
_____
_____
_____
_____
_____
_____
_____
_____
_____

What would I do better next time?

_____
_____
_____
_____
_____
_____
_____
_____
_____
_____
_____
_____
_____

┌─ The topic we discussed: ─────────┐ ┌─ Date ─┐
└───────────────────────────────────┘ └────────┘

Record your child(ren) response: Share your thoughts

_____   _____
_____   _____
_____   _____
_____   _____
_____   _____
_____   _____
_____   _____
_____   _____
_____   _____
_____   _____
_____   _____
_____   _____

What went well?   What didn't go well

_____   _____
_____   _____
_____   _____
_____   _____
_____   _____
_____   _____
_____   _____
_____   _____
_____   _____
_____   _____
_____   _____
_____   _____

What do you think God is saying about this topic?

_____
_____
_____
_____
_____
_____
_____
_____
_____
_____
_____
_____
_____

What have I learned about my child(ren)?

_____
_____
_____
_____
_____
_____
_____
_____
_____
_____
_____
_____
_____

What have I learned as a parent?

_____
_____
_____
_____
_____
_____
_____
_____
_____
_____
_____
_____
_____

What would I do better next time?

_____
_____
_____
_____
_____
_____
_____
_____
_____
_____
_____
_____
_____

| The topic we discussed: | Date |

Record your child(ren) response:

Share your thoughts

What went well?

What didn't go well

What do you think God is saying about this topic?

What have I learned about my child(ren)?

What have I learned as a parent?

What would I do better next time?

The topic we discussed: **Date**

Record your child(ren) response: Share your thoughts

_____   _____
_____   _____
_____   _____
_____   _____
_____   _____
_____   _____
_____   _____
_____   _____
_____   _____
_____   _____
_____   _____

What went well?   What didn't go well

_____   _____
_____   _____
_____   _____
_____   _____
_____   _____
_____   _____
_____   _____
_____   _____
_____   _____
_____   _____
_____   _____

What do you think God is saying about this topic?

_____
_____
_____
_____
_____
_____
_____
_____
_____
_____
_____
_____
_____

What have I learned about my child(ren)?

_____
_____
_____
_____
_____
_____
_____
_____
_____
_____
_____
_____
_____

What have I learned as a parent?

_____
_____
_____
_____
_____
_____
_____
_____
_____
_____
_____
_____
_____

What would I do better next time?

_____
_____
_____
_____
_____
_____
_____
_____
_____
_____
_____
_____
_____

| The topic we discussed: | Date |

Record your child(ren) response: Share your thoughts

What went well?   What didn't go well

What do you think God is saying about this topic?

_____
_____
_____
_____
_____
_____
_____
_____
_____
_____
_____
_____
_____

What have I learned about my child(ren)?

_____
_____
_____
_____
_____
_____
_____
_____
_____
_____
_____
_____
_____

What have I learned as a parent?

_____
_____
_____
_____
_____
_____
_____
_____
_____
_____
_____
_____
_____

What would I do better next time?

_____
_____
_____
_____
_____
_____
_____
_____
_____
_____
_____
_____
_____

The topic we discussed:	Date

Record your child(ren) response: Share your thoughts

_____   _____
_____   _____
_____   _____
_____   _____
_____   _____
_____   _____
_____   _____
_____   _____
_____   _____
_____   _____
_____   _____
_____   _____

What went well?   What didn't go well

_____   _____
_____   _____
_____   _____
_____   _____
_____   _____
_____   _____
_____   _____
_____   _____
_____   _____
_____   _____
_____   _____
_____   _____

What do you think God is saying about this topic?

_____
_____
_____
_____
_____
_____
_____
_____
_____
_____
_____
_____
_____

What have I learned about my child(ren)?

_____
_____
_____
_____
_____
_____
_____
_____
_____
_____
_____
_____
_____

What have I learned as a parent?

_____
_____
_____
_____
_____
_____
_____
_____
_____
_____
_____
_____
_____

What would I do better next time?

_____
_____
_____
_____
_____
_____
_____
_____
_____
_____
_____
_____
_____

The topic we discussed: | **Date**

Record your child(ren) response:

Share your thoughts

What went well?

What didn't go well

What do you think God is saying about this topic?	What have I learned about my child(ren)?

What have I learned as a parent?	What would I do better next time?

| The topic we discussed: | Date |
|---|---|ುu
| | |

Record your child(ren) response: Share your thoughts

What went well?   What didn't go well

What do you think God is saying about this topic?	What have I learned about my child(ren)?

What have I learned as a parent?	What would I do better next time?

The topic we discussed:

Date

Record your child(ren) response:

Share your thoughts

What went well?

What didn't go well

What do you think God is saying about this topic?

_____
_____
_____
_____
_____
_____
_____
_____
_____
_____
_____
_____

What have I learned about my child(ren)?

_____
_____
_____
_____
_____
_____
_____
_____
_____
_____
_____
_____

What have I learned as a parent?

_____
_____
_____
_____
_____
_____
_____
_____
_____
_____
_____
_____

What would I do better next time?

_____
_____
_____
_____
_____
_____
_____
_____
_____
_____
_____
_____

| The topic we discussed: | Date |

Record your child(ren) response:

Share your thoughts

What went well?

What didn't go well

What do you think God is saying about this topic?

What have I learned about my child(ren)?

What have I learned as a parent?

What would I do better next time?

The topic we discussed:	Date

Record your child(ren) response: Share your thoughts

_____ _____
_____ _____
_____ _____
_____ _____
_____ _____
_____ _____
_____ _____
_____ _____
_____ _____
_____ _____
_____ _____

What went well? What didn't go well

_____ _____
_____ _____
_____ _____
_____ _____
_____ _____
_____ _____
_____ _____
_____ _____
_____ _____
_____ _____
_____ _____

What do you think God is saying about this topic?

_____
_____
_____
_____
_____
_____
_____
_____
_____
_____
_____
_____
_____
_____

What have I learned about my child(ren)?

_____
_____
_____
_____
_____
_____
_____
_____
_____
_____
_____
_____
_____
_____

What have I learned as a parent?

_____
_____
_____
_____
_____
_____
_____
_____
_____
_____
_____
_____
_____
_____

What would I do better next time?

_____
_____
_____
_____
_____
_____
_____
_____
_____
_____
_____
_____
_____
_____

┌─ **The topic we discussed:** ─────────┐   ┌─ **Date** ─┐
│   │   │   │
└───────────────────────────────────────┘   └────────────┘

Record your child(ren) response: Share your thoughts

_____   _____
_____   _____
_____   _____
_____   _____
_____   _____
_____   _____
_____   _____
_____   _____
_____   _____
_____   _____
_____   _____
_____   _____

What went well?   What didn't go well

_____   _____
_____   _____
_____   _____
_____   _____
_____   _____
_____   _____
_____   _____
_____   _____
_____   _____
_____   _____
_____   _____
_____   _____

What do you think God is saying about this topic?	What have I learned about my child(ren)?

What have I learned as a parent?	What would I do better next time?

┌─ The topic we discussed: ─────────┐   ┌─ Date ─┐
│   │   │   │
└────────────────────────────────────┘   └────────┘

Record your child(ren) response: Share your thoughts

_____   _____
_____   _____
_____   _____
_____   _____
_____   _____
_____   _____
_____   _____
_____   _____
_____   _____
_____   _____
_____   _____

What went well?   What didn't go well

_____   _____
_____   _____
_____   _____
_____   _____
_____   _____
_____   _____
_____   _____
_____   _____
_____   _____
_____   _____
_____   _____

What do you think God is saying about this topic?

_____
_____
_____
_____
_____
_____
_____
_____
_____
_____
_____
_____

What have I learned about my child(ren)?

_____
_____
_____
_____
_____
_____
_____
_____
_____
_____
_____
_____

What have I learned as a parent?

_____
_____
_____
_____
_____
_____
_____
_____
_____
_____
_____
_____

What would I do better next time?

_____
_____
_____
_____
_____
_____
_____
_____
_____
_____
_____
_____

The topic we discussed: | Date

Record your child(ren) response: | Share your thoughts

What went well? | What didn't go well

What do you think God is saying about this topic?

_____
_____
_____
_____
_____
_____
_____
_____
_____
_____
_____
_____
_____

What have I learned about my child(ren)?

_____
_____
_____
_____
_____
_____
_____
_____
_____
_____
_____
_____
_____

What have I learned as a parent?

_____
_____
_____
_____
_____
_____
_____
_____
_____
_____
_____
_____
_____

What would I do better next time?

_____
_____
_____
_____
_____
_____
_____
_____
_____
_____
_____
_____
_____

The topic we discussed: **Date**

Record your child(ren) response:

Share your thoughts

What went well?

What didn't go well

What do you think God is saying about this topic?

_____
_____
_____
_____
_____
_____
_____
_____
_____
_____
_____
_____

What have I learned about my child(ren)?

_____
_____
_____
_____
_____
_____
_____
_____
_____
_____
_____
_____

What have I learned as a parent?

_____
_____
_____
_____
_____
_____
_____
_____
_____
_____
_____
_____

What would I do better next time?

_____
_____
_____
_____
_____
_____
_____
_____
_____
_____
_____
_____

The topic we discussed:	Date

Record your child(ren) response:

Share your thoughts

What went well?

What didn't go well

What do you think God is saying about this topic?

_____
_____
_____
_____
_____
_____
_____
_____
_____
_____
_____
_____
_____

What have I learned about my child(ren)?

_____
_____
_____
_____
_____
_____
_____
_____
_____
_____
_____
_____
_____

What have I learned as a parent?

_____
_____
_____
_____
_____
_____
_____
_____
_____
_____
_____
_____
_____

What would I do better next time?

_____
_____
_____
_____
_____
_____
_____
_____
_____
_____
_____
_____
_____

| The topic we discussed: | Date |

Record your child(ren) response:

Share your thoughts

What went well?

What didn't go well

What do you think God is saying about this topic?

_____
_____
_____
_____
_____
_____
_____
_____
_____
_____
_____
_____
_____

What have I learned about my child(ren)?

_____
_____
_____
_____
_____
_____
_____
_____
_____
_____
_____
_____
_____

What have I learned as a parent?

_____
_____
_____
_____
_____
_____
_____
_____
_____
_____
_____
_____
_____

What would I do better next time?

_____
_____
_____
_____
_____
_____
_____
_____
_____
_____
_____
_____
_____

The topic we discussed:	Date

Record your child(ren) response:

Share your thoughts

_____

What went well?

What didn't go well

What do you think God is saying about this topic?

_____
_____
_____
_____
_____
_____
_____
_____
_____
_____
_____
_____

What have I learned about my child(ren)?

_____
_____
_____
_____
_____
_____
_____
_____
_____
_____
_____
_____

What have I learned as a parent?

_____
_____
_____
_____
_____
_____
_____
_____
_____
_____
_____
_____

What would I do better next time?

_____
_____
_____
_____
_____
_____
_____
_____
_____
_____
_____
_____

The topic we discussed: **Date**

Record your child(ren) response:

Share your thoughts

What went well?

What didn't go well

What do you think God is saying about this topic?

_____
_____
_____
_____
_____
_____
_____
_____
_____
_____
_____
_____

What have I learned about my child(ren)?

_____
_____
_____
_____
_____
_____
_____
_____
_____
_____
_____
_____

What have I learned as a parent?

_____
_____
_____
_____
_____
_____
_____
_____
_____
_____
_____
_____

What would I do better next time?

_____
_____
_____
_____
_____
_____
_____
_____
_____
_____
_____
_____

The topic we discussed:

Date

Record your child(ren) response:

Share your thoughts

What went well?

What didn't go well

What do you think God is saying about this topic?

_____
_____
_____
_____
_____
_____
_____
_____
_____
_____
_____
_____

What have I learned about my child(ren)?

_____
_____
_____
_____
_____
_____
_____
_____
_____
_____
_____
_____

What have I learned as a parent?

_____
_____
_____
_____
_____
_____
_____
_____
_____
_____
_____
_____

What would I do better next time?

_____
_____
_____
_____
_____
_____
_____
_____
_____
_____
_____
_____

The topic we discussed:　　　　　　　　**Date**

Record your child(ren) response:　　　Share your thoughts

What went well?　　　　　　　　　What didn't go well

What do you think God is saying about this topic?

_____
_____
_____
_____
_____
_____
_____
_____
_____
_____
_____
_____

What have I learned about my child(ren)?

_____
_____
_____
_____
_____
_____
_____
_____
_____
_____
_____
_____

What have I learned as a parent?

_____
_____
_____
_____
_____
_____
_____
_____
_____
_____
_____
_____

What would I do better next time?

_____
_____
_____
_____
_____
_____
_____
_____
_____
_____
_____
_____

The topic we discussed: **Date**

Record your child(ren) response: Share your thoughts

What went well?   What didn't go well

What do you think God is saying about this topic?

_____
_____
_____
_____
_____
_____
_____
_____
_____
_____
_____
_____

What have I learned about my child(ren)?

_____
_____
_____
_____
_____
_____
_____
_____
_____
_____
_____
_____

What have I learned as a parent?

_____
_____
_____
_____
_____
_____
_____
_____
_____
_____
_____
_____

What would I do better next time?

_____
_____
_____
_____
_____
_____
_____
_____
_____
_____
_____
_____

The topic we discussed: | **Date**

Record your child(ren) response:

Share your thoughts

What went well?

What didn't go well

What do you think God is saying about this topic?	What have I learned about my child(ren)?

What have I learned as a parent?	What would I do better next time?

The topic we discussed: | **Date**

Record your child(ren) response:

Share your thoughts

What went well?

What didn't go well

What do you think God is saying about this topic?

_____
_____
_____
_____
_____
_____
_____
_____
_____
_____
_____
_____

What have I learned about my child(ren)?

_____
_____
_____
_____
_____
_____
_____
_____
_____
_____
_____
_____

What have I learned as a parent?

_____
_____
_____
_____
_____
_____
_____
_____
_____
_____
_____
_____

What would I do better next time?

_____
_____
_____
_____
_____
_____
_____
_____
_____
_____
_____
_____

| The topic we discussed: | Date |

Record your child(ren) response:

Share your thoughts

What went well?

What didn't go well

What do you think God is saying about this topic?	What have I learned about my child(ren)?

What have I learned as a parent?	What would I do better next time?

| The topic we discussed: | | Date |

Record your child(ren) response: Share your thoughts

What went well?   What didn't go well

What do you think God is saying about this topic?

_____
_____
_____
_____
_____
_____
_____
_____
_____
_____
_____
_____

What have I learned about my child(ren)?

_____
_____
_____
_____
_____
_____
_____
_____
_____
_____
_____
_____

What have I learned as a parent?

_____
_____
_____
_____
_____
_____
_____
_____
_____
_____
_____
_____

What would I do better next time?

_____
_____
_____
_____
_____
_____
_____
_____
_____
_____
_____
_____

| The topic we discussed: | Date |

Record your child(ren) response: Share your thoughts

What went well?   What didn't go well

What do you think God is saying about this topic?

_____
_____
_____
_____
_____
_____
_____
_____
_____
_____
_____
_____
_____
_____

What have I learned about my child(ren)?

_____
_____
_____
_____
_____
_____
_____
_____
_____
_____
_____
_____
_____
_____

What have I learned as a parent?

_____
_____
_____
_____
_____
_____
_____
_____
_____
_____
_____
_____
_____
_____

What would I do better next time?

_____
_____
_____
_____
_____
_____
_____
_____
_____
_____
_____
_____
_____
_____

The topic we discussed: | **Date**

Record your child(ren) response:

Share your thoughts

What went well?

What didn't go well

What do you think God is saying about this topic?

_____
_____
_____
_____
_____
_____
_____
_____
_____
_____
_____
_____
_____

What have I learned about my child(ren)?

_____
_____
_____
_____
_____
_____
_____
_____
_____
_____
_____
_____
_____

What have I learned as a parent?

_____
_____
_____
_____
_____
_____
_____
_____
_____
_____
_____
_____
_____

What would I do better next time?

_____
_____
_____
_____
_____
_____
_____
_____
_____
_____
_____
_____
_____

The topic we discussed:		Date

Record your child(ren) response:

_____
_____
_____
_____
_____
_____
_____
_____
_____
_____
_____
_____

Share your thoughts

_____
_____
_____
_____
_____
_____
_____
_____
_____
_____
_____
_____

What went well?

_____
_____
_____
_____
_____
_____
_____
_____
_____
_____
_____
_____

What didn't go well

_____
_____
_____
_____
_____
_____
_____
_____
_____
_____
_____
_____

What do you think God is saying about this topic?	What have I learned about my child(ren)?

What have I learned as a parent?	What would I do better next time?

Bonus pages to help you communicate, connect, and instruct your child(ren) on this journey

Communicate

HOW DID I COMMUNICATE THIS MONTH?

COMMUNICATE

How did I communicate with the children this month?

How am I an intentional parent in terms of communicating?

How do I feel about my intentional parenting journey?

Any changes? (In your life, or with the child(ren)

Scripture (write a scripture that speaks to you):

Prayer and Declaration (Say a prayer relative to the topic discussed or your concerns):

HOW DID I COMMUNICATE THIS MONTH?

COMMUNICATE

How did I communicate with the children this month?

How am I an intentional parent in terms of communicating?

How do I feel about my intentional parenting journey?

Any changes? (In your life, or with the child(ren)

Scripture (write a scripture that speaks to you):

Prayer and Declaration (Say a prayer relative to the topic discussed or your concerns):

HOW DID I COMMUNICATE THIS MONTH?

COMMUNICATE

How did I communicate with the children this month?

How am I an intentional parent in terms of communicating?

How do I feel about my intentional parenting journey?

Any changes? (In your life, or with the child(ren)

Scripture (write a scripture that speaks to you):

Prayer and Declaration (Say a prayer relative to the topic discussed or your concerns):

HOW DID I COMMUNICATE THIS MONTH?

COMMUNICATE

How did I communicate with the children this month?

How am I an intentional parent in terms of communicating?

How do I feel about my intentional parenting journey?

Any changes? (In your life, or with the child(ren)

Scripture (write a scripture that speaks to you):

Prayer and Declaration (Say a prayer relative to the topic discussed or your concerns):

HOW DID I COMMUNICATE THIS MONTH?

COMMUNICATE

How did I communicate with the children this month?

How am I an intentional parent in terms of communicating?

How do I feel about my intentional parenting journey?

Any changes? (In your life, or with the child(ren)

Scripture (write a scripture that speaks to you):

Prayer and Declaration (Say a prayer relative to the topic discussed or your concerns):

HOW DID I COMMUNICATE THIS MONTH?

COMMUNICATE

How did I communicate with the children this month?

How am I an intentional parent in terms of communicating?

How do I feel about my intentional parenting journey?

Any changes? (In your life, or with the child(ren)

Scripture (write a scripture that speaks to you):

Prayer and Declaration (Say a prayer relative to the topic discussed or your concerns):

HOW DID I COMMUNICATE THIS MONTH?

COMMUNICATE

How did I communicate with the children this month?

How am I an intentional parent in terms of communicating?

How do I feel about my intentional parenting journey?

Any changes? (In your life, or with the child(ren)

Scripture (write a scripture that speaks to you):

Prayer and Declaration (Say a prayer relative to the topic discussed or your concerns):

HOW DID I COMMUNICATE THIS MONTH?

COMMUNICATE

How did I communicate with the children this month?

How am I an intentional parent in terms of communicating?

How do I feel about my intentional parenting journey?

Any changes? (In your life, or with the child(ren)

Scripture (write a scripture that speaks to you):

Prayer and Declaration (Say a prayer relative to the topic discussed or your concerns):

HOW DID I COMMUNICATE THIS MONTH?

COMMUNICATE

How did I communicate with the children this month?

How am I an intentional parent in terms of communicating?

How do I feel about my intentional parenting journey?

Any changes? (In your life, or with the child(ren)

Scripture (write a scripture that speaks to you):

Prayer and Declaration (Say a prayer relative to the topic discussed or your concerns):

HOW DID I COMMUNICATE THIS MONTH?

COMMUNICATE

How did I communicate with the children this month?

How am I an intentional parent in terms of communicating?

How do I feel about my intentional parenting journey?

Any changes? (In your life, or with the child(ren)

Scripture (write a scripture that speaks to you):

Prayer and Declaration (Say a prayer relative to the topic discussed or your concerns):

HOW DID I COMMUNICATE THIS MONTH?

COMMUNICATE

How did I communicate with the children this month?

How am I an intentional parent in terms of communicating?

How do I feel about my intentional parenting journey?

Any changes? (In your life, or with the child(ren)

Scripture (write a scripture that speaks to you):

Prayer and Declaration (Say a prayer relative to the topic discussed or your concerns):

HOW DID I COMMUNICATE THIS MONTH?

COMMUNICATE

How did I communicate with the children this month?

How am I an intentional parent in terms of communicating?

How do I feel about my intentional parenting journey?

Any changes? (In your life, or with the child(ren)

Scripture (write a scripture that speaks to you):

Prayer and Declaration (Say a prayer relative to the topic discussed or your concerns):

Connect

HOW DID I CONNECT THIS MONTH?

CONNECT

How did I connect this month?

How am I being an intentional parent connecting with my child(ren) this month?

What activities did we do to connect as a family or with the children?

Any changes? (In your life, or with the child(ren)

Scripture (write a scripture that speaks to you):

Prayer and Declaration (Say a prayer relative to the topic discussed or your concerns):

HOW DID I CONNECT THIS MONTH?

CONNECT

How did I connect this month?

How am I being an intentional parent connecting with my child(ren) this month?

What activities did we do to connect as a family or with the children?

Any changes? (In your life, or with the child(ren)

Scripture (write a scripture that speaks to you):

Prayer and Declaration (Say a prayer relative to the topic discussed or your concerns):

HOW DID I CONNECT THIS MONTH?

CONNECT

How did I connect this month?

How am I being an intentional parent connecting with my child(ren) this month?

What activities did we do to connect as a family or with the children?

Any changes? (In your life, or with the child(ren)

Scripture (write a scripture that speaks to you):

Prayer and Declaration (Say a prayer relative to the topic discussed or your concerns):

HOW DID I CONNECT THIS MONTH?

CONNECT

How did I connect this month?

How am I being an intentional parent connecting with my child(ren) this month?

What activities did we do to connect as a family or with the children?

Any changes? (In your life, or with the child(ren)

Scripture (write a scripture that speaks to you):

Prayer and Declaration (Say a prayer relative to the topic discussed or your concerns):

HOW DID I CONNECT THIS MONTH?

CONNECT

How did I connect this month?

How am I being an intentional parent connecting with my child(ren) this month?

What activities did we do to connect as a family or with the children?

___Any changes? (In your life, or with the child(ren) ___

___Scripture (write a scripture that speaks to you): ___

___Prayer and Declaration (Say a prayer relative to the topic discussed or your concerns): ___

HOW DID I CONNECT THIS MONTH?

CONNECT

How did I connect this month?

How am I being an intentional parent connecting with my child(ren) this month?

What activities did we do to connect as a family or with the children?

Any changes? (In your life, or with the child(ren)

Scripture (write a scripture that speaks to you):

Prayer and Declaration (Say a prayer relative to the topic discussed or your concerns):

HOW DID I CONNECT THIS MONTH?

CONNECT

How did I connect this month?

How am I being an intentional parent connecting with my child(ren) this month?

What activities did we do to connect as a family or with the children?

Any changes? (In your life, or with the child(ren)

Scripture (write a scripture that speaks to you):

Prayer and Declaration (Say a prayer relative to the topic discussed or your concerns):

HOW DID I CONNECT THIS MONTH?

CONNECT

How did I connect this month?

How am I being an intentional parent connecting with my child(ren) this month?

What activities did we do to connect as a family or with the children?

Any changes? (In your life, or with the child(ren)

Scripture (write a scripture that speaks to you):

Prayer and Declaration (Say a prayer relative to the topic discussed or your concerns):

HOW DID I CONNECT THIS MONTH?

CONNECT

How did I connect this month?

How am I being an intentional parent connecting with my child(ren) this month?

What activities did we do to connect as a family or with the children?

____Any changes? (In your life, or with the child(ren)

____Scripture (write a scripture that speaks to you):

____Prayer and Declaration (Say a prayer relative to the topic discussed or your concerns):

HOW DID I CONNECT THIS MONTH?

CONNECT

How did I connect this month?

How am I being an intentional parent connecting with my child(ren) this month?

What activities did we do to connect as a family or with the children?

Any changes? (In your life, or with the child(ren)

Scripture (write a scripture that speaks to you):

Prayer and Declaration (Say a prayer relative to the topic discussed or your concerns):

HOW DID I CONNECT THIS MONTH?

CONNECT

How did I connect this month?

How am I being an intentional parent connecting with my child(ren) this month?

What activities did we do to connect as a family or with the children?

Any changes? (In your life, or with the child(ren)

Scripture (write a scripture that speaks to you):

Prayer and Declaration (Say a prayer relative to the topic discussed or your concerns):

HOW DID I CONNECT THIS MONTH?

CONNECT

How did I connect this month?

How am I being an intentional parent connecting with my child(ren) this month?

What activities did we do to connect as a family or with the children?

Any changes? (In your life, or with the child(ren)

Scripture (write a scripture that speaks to you):

Prayer and Declaration (Say a prayer relative to the topic discussed or your concerns):

Instruct & Equip

HOW DID I INSTRUCT & EQUIP THIS MONTH?

INSTRUCT & EQUIP

How did I instruct & equip my child(ren) this month?

What activities, classes, or camps did they sign up for?

What new skills did they learn?

Any new interests, hobbies, or affinities?

How are you feeding that interest, passion, or hobby?

Set new instructional goals and include a timeline

HOW DID I INSTRUCT & EQUIP THIS MONTH?

INSTRUCT & EQUIP

How did I instruct & equip my child(ren) this month?

What activities, classes, or camps did they sign up for?

What new skills did they learn?

Any new interests, hobbies, or affinities?

How are you feeding that interest, passion, or hobby?

Set new instructional goals and include a timeline

HOW DID I INSTRUCT & EQUIP THIS MONTH?

INSTRUCT & EQUIP

How did I instruct & equip my child(ren) this month?

What activities, classes, or camps did they sign up for?

What new skills did they learn?

Any new interests, hobbies, or affinities?

How are you feeding that interest, passion, or hobby?

Set new instructional goals and include a timeline

HOW DID I INSTRUCT & EQUIP THIS MONTH?

INSTRUCT & EQUIP

How did I instruct & equip my child(ren) this month?

What activities, classes, or camps did they sign up for?

What new skills did they learn?

Any new interests, hobbies, or affinities?

How are you feeding that interest, passion, or hobby?

Set new instructional goals and include a timeline

HOW DID I INSTRUCT & EQUIP THIS MONTH?

INSTRUCT & EQUIP

How did I instruct & equip my child(ren) this month?

What activities, classes, or camps did they sign up for?

What new skills did they learn?

Any new interests, hobbies, or affinities?

How are you feeding that interest, passion, or hobby?

Set new instructional goals and include a timeline

HOW DID I INSTRUCT & EQUIP THIS MONTH?

INSTRUCT & EQUIP

How did I instruct & equip my child(ren) this month?

What activities, classes, or camps did they sign up for?

What new skills did they learn?

Any new interests, hobbies, or affinities?

How are you feeding that interest, passion, or hobby?

Set new instructional goals and include a timeline

HOW DID I INSTRUCT & EQUIP THIS MONTH?

INSTRUCT & EQUIP

How did I instruct & equip my child(ren) this month?

What activities, classes, or camps did they sign up for?

What new skills did they learn?

Any new interests, hobbies, or affinities?

How are you feeding that interest, passion, or hobby?

Set new instructional goals and include a timeline

HOW DID I INSTRUCT & EQUIP THIS MONTH?

INSTRUCT & EQUIP

How did I instruct & equip my child(ren) this month?

What activities, classes, or camps did they sign up for?

What new skills did they learn?

Any new interests, hobbies, or affinities?

How are you feeding that interest, passion, or hobby?

Set new instructional goals and include a timeline

HOW DID I INSTRUCT & EQUIP THIS MONTH?

INSTRUCT & EQUIP

How did I instruct & equip my child(ren) this month?

What activities, classes, or camps did they sign up for?

What new skills did they learn?

Any new interests, hobbies, or affinities?

How are you feeding that interest, passion, or hobby?

Set new instructional goals and include a timeline

HOW DID I INSTRUCT & EQUIP THIS MONTH?

INSTRUCT & EQUIP

How did I instruct & equip my child(ren) this month?

What activities, classes, or camps did they sign up for?

What new skills did they learn?

Any new interests, hobbies, or affinities?

How are you feeding that interest, passion, or hobby?

Set new instructional goals and include a timeline

HOW DID I INSTRUCT & EQUIP THIS MONTH?

INSTRUCT & EQUIP

How did I instruct & equip my child(ren) this month?

What activities, classes, or camps did they sign up for?

What new skills did they learn?

Any new interests, hobbies, or affinities?

How are you feeding that interest, passion, or hobby?

Set new instructional goals and include a timeline

HOW DID I INSTRUCT & EQUIP THIS MONTH?

INSTRUCT & EQUIP

How did I instruct & equip my child(ren) this month?

What activities, classes, or camps did they sign up for?

What new skills did they learn?

Any new interests, hobbies, or affinities?

How are you feeding that interest, passion, or hobby?

Set new instructional goals and include a timeline

Notes

www.ingramcontent.com/pod-product-compliance
Lightning Source LLC
Chambersburg PA
CBHW042047280426
43673CB00076B/263